OWN YOUR CAREER

TAKE CONTROL +
ACCELERATE YOUR
PROFESSIONAL GROWTH

Annette Garsteck

Author Name
Annette Garsteck

Publisher Name
Annette Garsteck Career Consulting LLC

Contact Information
Annette Garsteck, Annette Garsteck Career Consulting LLC
ownyourcareer@annettegarsteck.com

Own Your Career: Take Control + Accelerate Your Professional Growth / Annette Garsteck—1st ed.
ISBN 979-8-9924289-8-8

CONTENTS

This book is dedicated to all the women who want more for themselves, their careers, and the lives they impact.

INTRODUCTION

You should be so proud of yourself!

You picked up this book, demonstrating how invested you are in personal and professional growth. You want to do the work to grow your mindset, deepen your skills, and expand what is possible for you in your career. I am here to guide you through doing just that! I want this book to make a real difference in your career.

No one can be more invested in your career growth than you.

Have you ever thought, "If I keep my head down and work hard, someone will notice me? " or "I'll volunteer for this project so my boss will see how dedicated I am to the company?"

If you said yes, I understand, and you are not alone. I've had these same thoughts myself, a time or two. I guarantee you that these thoughts are not sustainable career development plans, and they will not land you a promotion.

To have a meaningful career, one you are proud of, you must do more than wait for someone to finally notice you and then tap you on the shoulder and offer you the job you want or your desired promotion. It is up to you.

Only you can:

- Reflect and decide what you desire for the next phase of your career
- Develop and deepen your professional skills
- Do the mindset work to find out what gets you excited about your future
- Research to understand your value in the overall job market
- Grow your circle of influence
- Record, recognize, and speak about attaining your unique accomplishments

You can invest in these areas regardless of your job title, whether you have been in your job for five weeks or five years, and even if you aren't doing the type of job you envisioned when you graduated. Or you work in a different industry than you dreamed.

Developing a positive mindset and success-focused habits will carry you through life, in general, not just your professional life.

I wasn't always a certified career coach. In fact, I first built a successful career in corporate America. I am proud to say that most of my opportunities resulted from my professional reputation, a personal brand of effectiveness, knowledge, and reliability, and my circle of connections.

My corporate, and first, career was not linear, traditional, or even expected. It started when I swapped my full-time college education during my sophomore year for a full-time job. I pursued my education while I worked and leveraged my tuition reimbursement benefits to keep me debt-free. I transitioned from a temporary worker to a full-time employee. Then, I worked myself up the ranks, experiencing inside and outside sales, training new hires, and eventually leading a team of inside sales professionals. I loved my leadership role and earned a President's Club trip when my team members achieved their key performance indicators (KPIs) and our team goals.

Do you want to know what I consider the highlight of the experience? It wasn't the trip (as you might expect—Hawaii). It was helping my direct reports achieve their career goals! I used the knowledge gained at two Fortune 50 organizations to guide my team members on résumés, cover letters, interview best practices, and negotiation tactics when transitioning to an internal role or leaving the company for a new challenge.

Teaching others what it takes to change roles, be promoted, and have a fulfilling career was a theme in my work. No matter what organization I worked in, I managed to help my team, peers, and co-workers transition to their next set of career aspirations.

When I left my first full-time job, I knew that my career path was only limited by my imagination. I used the skills I had developed to keep my résumé updated, stayed in touch with my valuable network connections, and reviewed every opportunity as it arrived. I made company and role changes when it added value to my career story or helped me increase my professional career worth. Now, I am excited to share with you the practices I developed and used to grow and advance my career.

I wholeheartedly trust that nurturing your career management and development skills is the way to take and maintain control of your professional path. It is how you can accelerate the time to be seen as operating in your zone of genius. It is an essential way you can own your career.

First, in this book, I will help you lay the foundation of key best practices. These activities can be done quickly and will help you achieve professional wins in and out of the office. These core habits are the things that I do each weekday (at a minimum). These habits helped me build a corporate career I was proud of and now a small business that allows me to work with you.

After you master the foundational habits, you will move to the build + grow habits and end with the leveling up habits. You won't be doing it alone; I will walk you through the process and offer encouragement and ideas to help you customize the concepts to match your unique style.

You've taken a courageous step toward your future self, and I'm excited to walk alongside you.

Keep going!

One important note before you start: this book does not address all the adversities women face in the workforce. These forces are undeniable. Women are penalized, omitted, and treated with bias in the workforce. There are too many systems of oppression, double standards, and biases that we encounter—to name only a few: sexism, ageism, discrimination, the glass ceiling, the glass wall, the broken rung, the double bind, the gender pay gap, and harassment. Often, the intersections of our many identities can limit our opportunities instead of being recognized as our overwhelming strengths.

We are socialized to be polite and accommodating, and then the invisible work in all the spaces we occupy is heaped on top of us. These are real obstacles to career success. I want to acknowledge these systemic wrongs and honor all the women who navigate these failings...every day. I know that women are infinitely powerful. I also know that to harness our collective strength, we must own it. In this book, I focus on empowering women, at first individually and then in community, to build consistent habits that support their career aspirations.

If you are ready, let's start now.

HOW TO USE THIS BOOK

I wrote this book to help you develop better habits in your professional career. This book has three sections: foundational habits, habits that help you build + grow in your career, and habits that will help you level up in your field. Each section will have five development areas to guide you in establishing new growth habits including, personal development, know your worth, mindset, accomplishment, and circle of influence.

Let's explore each of the five development areas we will focus on in this book.

Personal Development

Wikipedia defines personal development as "activities that develop a person's capabilities and potential, build human capital, facilitate employability, enhance quality of life, and facilitate the realization of dreams and aspirations."[i] I 100% agree! I will share a few methods to help you develop your potential, make you more valuable as an employee, and challenge your mind.

Knowing Your Worth

Understanding your unique value is no small undertaking. I will recommend action steps to help you realize your value in the market, define your role, track industry trends, and communicate your worth with impactful stories. This area is universally tricky for most women, so I look forward to processing it alongside you and helping you change your inner narrative around your worth.

Mindset

Improving your mindset is a concept that has made its way into our everyday conversations. I characterize mindset as steps you can practice to handle yourself gently, recognize the progress you are making, and view the future in a positive light. I will teach you a few of the practices I use to think about possibilities and how I open myself to receive new opportunities I hadn't previously considered.

Accomplishment

The things you get done in a day amaze me! The story you may tell yourself about accomplishment is probably different. That's okay. We will work on recognizing your accomplishments, recording them, and using the results for your benefit.

Circle of Influence

We cannot reach our fullest potential without the help of others, and yet asking for help can be a difficult thing to do. In this development area, we will explore how to nurture your existing circle, expand your network, and surround yourself with those that support your growth and goals.

Ready to get started? Grab a fresh notebook or fancy journal to record and practice your new habits. If you are more of a digital tracker, feel free to use a notes app or a Google Doc on your favorite device.

There is no wrong way to start. Taking action will help you develop new habits. Promise me that you won't judge the quality of your actions. Messy and imperfect action is superior to inaction. A note here about mistakes and failures: they do not define you. Doing it wrong will allow you to gather the data to decide what to tweak and adjust. Perfection will keep you stuck, and messy action will allow you to adapt and keep moving forward. Learn to embrace action as a beneficial part of growing and stepping up into the next level of your life.

Take one action every day. Keep taking that one action for five days out of the week. Stack the next habit on top of it. Stack one of the new habits you learn in this book with an already-existing habit you act on daily. This approach will help you develop habits that will become second nature.

I can vouch for this approach; I no longer think about purposefully fitting in my personal development time. I listen to audiobooks while driving or styling my hair. The mobile apps make it easy to add notes or bookmark clips that inspire me. After completing the book, I record it on my Goodreads list.

You, too, can develop practices that will support your growth and progress in your career.

I have designed an *Own Your Career* resource portal to accompany this book. To access it now, scan the QR code below.

SECTION ONE

FOUNDATIONAL HABITS

FOUNDATIONAL HABITS

No matter where you are in your professional life, you can build (or rebuild) practices that support your development and growth.

Have you recently graduated from school and landed your first "real" job?

Are you pivoting to a new industry and leaving your old career behind?

Are you re-entering the workforce after a gap caring for yourself or loved ones?

Have you been in your job for some time but want more for yourself?

No matter where you are in your career, this section is for you! Developing strong professional habits will help you create a solid foundation for future growth, help you build confidence, and get you excited, again, about learning.

Grab your journal, and let's get started!

FOUNDATIONAL HABITS
MINDSET
PRACTICE GRATITUDE

S elf-talk is the continuous loop of your inner voice. The voice that you always hear. According to Psychology Today, this voice has the power to "be cheerful and supportive or negative and self-defeating." [ii]

Your inner voice shapes how you feel about anything and everything. To mold those thoughts to see opportunity and positivity, practice gratitude daily. Gratitude is not a practice saved for special occasions. Daily gratitude has helped me realize I already have so much abundance in my life.

How do you start practicing gratitude? Write down one thing that you are thankful for. The next day, write down two things. Work up to writing five things you are grateful for every day. Your list can be the same every day. Or you can create a list of five unique things you appreciate daily.

Need some ideas to spur this new gratitude practice? I got you!

Consider using one of these prompts to get started.

- I am grateful for these two people in my family...
- I am grateful for this item in my home...
- I am grateful for the mentorship of...
- I am grateful for working with...
- I am grateful for this project at work...

After successfully writing about whom or what you are grateful for, I want you to go deeper and get specific. Why are you grateful for your family members? What does that video doorbell do for you that makes you so thankful? See where I am going with this?

At the end of every week, review the gratitude list. Recognize that you have much to be thankful for and that so many wonderful people support you. This is the best part of my week, and it keeps my optimism and positivity high!

FOUNDATIONAL HABITS
PERSONAL DEVELOPMENT
READ

There are so many ways to learn new things and expand your mind. No matter what level of formal education you have achieved, you can continue to build your level of knowledge by reading. Reading has so many benefits that help you in the workplace, including increasing your vocabulary and comprehension, empowering you to empathize with other people, and reducing stress.[iii]

Reading doesn't only mean books. You could read articles, blog posts, studies, white papers, company newsletters, magazines, or books. And yes, audiobooks count!

Decide how much time you will dedicate to reading each week. Spread this total time out over a few days. For example, if you want to read for an hour, you should schedule four-15-minute or three-20-minute sessions to achieve your new goal.

Now, decide what you will read. Do you have six articles saved on LinkedIn? Is there a stack of research sitting on your desk? What is on your Goodreads 'To Read' list?

Decide where you will read. Do you have a cozy nook at home? Do you like to read in a bustling coffeehouse? You may have a secret park where you can enjoy nature too. There is no wrong answer here.

If you are using the magic of audiobooks, you can "read" while working out, driving to the office, or cooking your breakfast.

Map it out in your notebook, and for good measure, write down one key thing you learned from what you read. Decide who you will share that key learning with for an extra level of accountability.

To gain some inspiration, I invite you to access my past reading lists and stay on track with me as I continue to read at least one book a week through the *Own Your Career* resource portal. Scan the QR code below to start now.

FOUNDATIONAL HABITS
CIRCLE OF INFLUENCE
NURTURE RELATIONSHIPS

Networking is an activity we've been told we should do regularly. Even daily. But it can feel a little forced if we don't know exactly how to start or what to do. Right? What if I told you networking meant establishing and nurturing connections with others?

Does this new definition make networking:

- Less intimidating?
- Less cringe-worthy?
- Less likely for you to postpone doing it?

What if you were maintaining contact with existing connections every day? Your impact on others and their impact on you would be positive and surpass your expectations.

To build this foundational habit, first focus on nurturing existing relationships.

Stay connected to the essential people in your life! To name a few, family, friends, current co-workers, clients, and vendors. Don't forget about people you know from previous jobs, college, high school, or grade school. Your network can also include your children's teachers, coaches, and friends' parents.

The best way to maintain this network of people is to stay in contact with them. Here are three options to help you strengthen existing relationships.

Have under five minutes? Make a quick contact.

- Send a text or voice note
- Connect on social media, comment on a post, or send a direct message
- Write an email
- Friend, follow or connect with them on their preferred social media channels to stay updated on their day-to-day

Have more time, maybe 10 minutes?

- Make a phone call - if you get their voicemail, leave a message
- Schedule a video chat
- Send a card via snail mail

Want to deepen that connection?

- Spend in-person time
- Schedule an experience, such as a manicure or movie outing
- Have coffee
- Go to lunch
- Get your heart pumping with a trip to the gym or a wellness class
- Have an outside adventure
- Attend a concert

Reach out to five people daily using a five-minute or less quick contact activity (or come up with one of your own). The goal is to restart the conversation with five people you already know at least five days a week. Keep track of them in your journal.

FOUNDATIONAL HABITS
ACCOMPLISHMENT
TRACKING SUCCESSES

"**W**omen attribute their success to working hard, luck, and help from other people. Men will attribute that - whatever success they have, that same success - to their own core skills." -Sheryl Sandberg[iv]

Does that quote resonate with you? You've probably told your leadership team that a project was a success because of the whole team. You may have said more than once that you did well because you were "lucky." When you were in an interview, I am sure you used the word "we" more than "I" or "me."

No doubt, women work hard, have support from other great team members, and have had their fair share of fortune. But that is only part of the story. You work more than 2,000 hours a year. There is more to your professional success than the story you tell yourself about luck and really wonderful co-workers.

Keeping a success file will stop the cycle of new successes overshadowing past accomplishments. You will build this evidence that you are more than "lucky," boosting your confidence at work.

Let's start with what already exists.

Collect your previous performance reviews. If they exist electronically in your firm's HRIS system, log in and print them out.

Find those monthly scorecards. The ones that tell you you've met or exceeded KPIs. If they are stored digitally, screenshot them or print them out.

Next, take these records home with you. These are yours to keep; they talk about your accomplishments and contain specific feedback about your performance. They are yours!

Look through your work email inbox for notes recognizing your unique talents and skills. I am talking about the messages that make you feel all warm and fuzzy when reading them. To clarify what you could find in your email archives, ask yourself questions like these:

- What kudos or compliments have I received?
- Did a client recognize any of my advanced competencies or skills?
- Was I featured in any company literature (newsletter, email, success story)?
- Was I nominated for or recognized with any company, volunteer or education awards?
- Did I train or mentor a new hire?
- What work-sponsored volunteerism have I participated in?
- Did a colleague or another department request to work with me?
- Was I asked to speak or make a presentation to senior leadership?
- Did I participate in professional development programs? Employee resource groups?

Wow, look at all your documented accomplishments! Take them in. Read them out loud. Post them on your refrigerator. Share them with a friend or family member. Internalize all this positive feedback.

To keep up on tracking all of your accomplishments, add a weekly reminder to your calendar and spend 15 minutes adding your weekly acknowledgments from others to your new success file.

Going forward, add one thing to your journal that you did well each day. This can be something small, like meeting a daily goal. Or it can be something significant, like nailing that client presentation and winning the account (congrats!).

Add a reminder to your calendar at the end of each workday to record a daily success in your journal.

**FOUNDATIONAL HABITS
KNOW YOUR WORTH
CALCULATE IT**

One of my favorite images says, "Know your worth, then add tax." Feeling undervalued and underpaid fuels resentment toward your work. Knowing that the new hire next to you is paid more than you and your five years of experience can be aggravating. Being told there has been no budget for merit increases for years is taking a toll on your career.

Many women do not know what they are worth in the job market. Let's end that right now...with you!

Finding your worth is a combination of research steps. Let's walk through them together.

Start with your current role and company:

1.   What is your current job title?
2.   What is your current salary?
3.   What is your current salary range? Include the minimum and maximum.
4.   Are you compensated closer to the range's minimum, mid-point, or maximum?
5.   How long have you been in this role?
6.   What is your highest education level?
7.   Have you earned any additional certifications, licenses or furthered your education?

Conduct pay research on some well-known resources:

1. What does Salary.com say your role is worth?
2. What does Payscale.com value your role at?
3. What does Glassdoor.com assign as an annual salary for your role?
4. While researching the sites above or others like them, examine the roles and responsibilities of similar or more senior job titles and note the salary range for each.

Look for current job vacancies:

1. Use LinkedIn to search for open roles with similar titles to yours that share salary data.
2. Search for your job title in locations that have passed pay transparency laws and are disclosing pay ranges for posted jobs.

You have collected a lot of information already! Let's evaluate it.

If you are a spreadsheet-type person, you have all the information neatly organized. If you are like me, you have some handwritten notes. Either is great. Collect the above research and evaluate your standing. Record where you are now and compare it to what you found. Answer the following questions:

▪   Are you paid at your full market value at your current organization?
▪   Is your title aligned with what is expected of you in your role?
▪   Is there a different job title that better explains your job responsibilities?
▪   Are you happy with your current company's valuation of you?

- Now that you have this information, what will you do with it?

Isn't it eye-opening to see where you are at? And to know what is possible for your potential compensation range and current title. Continue reflecting on what this information means for you. Consider what possible courses of action are available to you now.

You did it! You started building your foundational habit muscles, including growing a positive mindset, developing knowledge, nurturing meaningful relationships, tracking successes, and calculating your worth. Striving to take action in these areas on weekdays will allow you to see what you are accomplishing and how you are growing. Your self-concept and confidence will improve, helping you build your desired career.

SECTION TWO

BUILD + GROW
HABITS

Own Your Career

BUILD + GROW HABITS

Whoo Hoo! You have laid a super solid foundation! So far, you have incorporated gratitude into your days, are expanding your mind with new information, nurturing important relationships, and tracking your accomplishments. You've even calculated your market worth.

Now, it's time to dig deeper. In this section, we will focus on building new practices from the foundational ones you've recently mastered. You will grow and learn how you can invest in yourself, quantify success, and expand the size of your network. Ready to get started? I knew you'd say that!

BUILD + GROW HABITS
MINDSET
AFFIRMATIONS

It's very possible to walk into your future believing in yourself and your capabilities. But how?

Use positive affirmations! Does this sound a little "woo-woo?" Nope! It's science.

An article on PositivePsychology.com says that continued use of affirmations have been linked to decreases in stress, improvements in academic achievement, and lower rates of rumination. I'm sure you can benefit from all of these good things.[v]

So, what is an affirmation? It's a positive statement you say or write daily.

To craft an effective and positive affirmation. Include these three elements:

1. Write the statement in the first person.
2. Write or speak the affirmation statement in the present tense.
3. The statement(s) should reflect your core values or what is important to you.

You can create your own affirmations or use ones that feel true to you.

Here are some positive affirmations you can use to build a consistent new mindset practice.

- I believe in myself.
- I am confident.
- My work fulfills me.
- I am capable and successful.
- I am allowed to meet and exceed my expectations of myself.

Part of my morning routine is writing a positive affirmation five times in my journal. When I need extra stress relief, I thumb through the journal, absorbing the positivity. It helps center me. I hope this practice does the same for you.

Now, move to your journal, notebook, or digital tablet and write a positive affirmation for yourself. Write it again and again. Write it five times in total. As you are writing it, believe what you are saying to yourself. Envision yourself in the reality of the affirmation. Feels good, doesn't it?

Bonus tip: Layer this affirmation practice on top of your gratitude habit and watch your mindset shift to more positivity and self-assurance.

BUILD + GROW HABITS
PERSONAL DEVELOPMENT
INVEST IN YOURSELF

nvesting in your professional development has many benefits, including, but not limited to, meeting industry requirements, career advancement, expanding your skill set, leadership growth, and increased earning potential. Investing in yourself can take a variety of forms. Let's start with the no-cost investments that require only your time.

Attend the learning events your company sponsors. These events can help you learn about your company, products, industry, and the clients you serve. Register and attend as many of the following events as time allows:

- Lunch + Learns
- Company earnings meetings
- Customer discussion panels
- Industry expert talks
- Product or service demonstrations

Join an employee or business resource group. These communities unite to provide education, solve business problems, promote mentoring and cross-functional connection.

Participate in company-sponsored community involvement projects. These allow you to do good while you connect with colleagues, philanthropy partners, and local community members. Select events that align with your values and give extra meaning to your role.

Find industry panels, discussions, or training sessions. There are many free options offered online. You can sign up to be included on email lists or check out Eventbrite or Meetup to locate in-person and virtual event options.

There are also free online learning or certificate programs. I recommend investigating options such as LinkedIn Learning, Google Career Certificates, HubSpot, and Harvard University for such possibilities. LinkedIn Learning is often free to access through your local library, without leaving your cozy home office.

Ready for the next step?

Select two of these learning options to complete every month. Jot them in your journal. Return to your notes and write a recap for yourself after you complete it. Share key findings with your colleagues or work groups.

BUILD + GROW HABITS
KNOW YOUR WORTH
RESEARCH + JOB ALERTS

D efining your value in the marketplace is an evolving and continuous process. With the recent pay transparency legislation in New York, California, Colorado, and at least five more states in 2025, pay ranges for open roles will be posted and more readily available than ever before. There is so much power in having information.

Accessing this information can be easy if you automate it. Set up and leverage job alerts for this task! Yep, even if you aren't an active job seeker right now, you can use these job posting alerts to stay on top of trends, market conditions, and important salary data collection.

Five tips for setting up these alerts:

- Set up a weekly digest alert so you don't receive an overwhelming amount of information.
- Set up alerts for your current job title and any qualifier variations you can think of (such as senior or associate).
- Cast a wide net by setting nationwide alerts for your current title and its variations.
- Create an email box filter for these messages so they're ready for you when you go through them.
- Make space in your schedule weekly to review this incoming data.

Set a timer for 25 minutes right now and establish the alerts using the tips provided above. Go ahead, I'll wait for you!

All done? Welcome back! Now, let's discuss what to do with the information you receive and how to leverage it to understand your worth.

Reserve 25 to 40 minutes each week to review this information. The 25 and 40-minute durations are part of the Pomodoro Technique, a time management strategy I swear by when trying to be super-productive. I highly recommend it to you. Don't overcomplicate this scheduling. It could be while you're in your car waiting to pick somebody up, during the lunch hour one day of the week, or on Saturday while enjoying your first cup of coffee.

Next, look through the job alerts. What interests you and why? Make notes. Avoid judging the roles, listing all the reasons you aren't qualified, or writing it off because it's not a fully remote role. You are collecting data. The most critical data point you are looking for is the salary range.

Let's discuss recording this vital information. If you're a spreadsheet person, go ahead and make a spreadsheet. If you still love the ceremony of writing something by hand, record it in your journal or notebook. Where you record it doesn't matter to me, but it will matter to you, so pick a place and stick with it. You want it to be easy to access.

This exercise will yield a few outcomes. First is a new language to discuss your duties, tasks, and accomplishments with words outside of your company's current lexicon. Cut and paste any interesting information into another document because these posted jobs can disappear anytime. Record the names and types of companies with this role available when you are ready to launch a future job search.

Second, you will have actual salary ranges offered by real companies to compare to the data you collected during the Foundational Habits section of the book from Payscale.com or Salary.com. What do you notice about how this role relates to the range? And if the ranges seem off, why is this job title not aligned with your current work?

Third, you have collected data you can return to when completing your annual review self-assessment, negotiating a promotion offer, or considering launching a job search.

Review the information each month and reflect on these questions. Are you noticing a pattern? Are you severely underpaid? How do your current responsibilities align with these roles? Now that you have this data, how do you feel about it?

This reflection work matters, and I'd love to hear from you about your findings. Please send me an email at ownyourcareer@annettegarsteck.com and let me know a highlight. What is this information showing you about your worth? Is it reinforcing a belief or making you rethink your value at work?

BUILD + GROW HABITS
ACCOMPLISHMENT
QUANTIFY SUCCESS

E arly in this Own Your Career process, you started tracking your success. Every day, you noted something that you did that was a positive outcome in your day. Now, let's expand on that habit.

There are many professional successes you can experience. You may have completed your part of a group project, you reached a monthly goal early, or you won an award. These are amazing as individual accomplishments or as a collection of actions.

To make this list of wins more robust, consider tracking their depth and quantifying their level of impact on your organization.

How do you do that?

Look at your list of accomplishments and ask yourself questions like:

- How many?
- When? How often?
- What was the goal?
- How did I measure against the plan?
- Was there an improvement?
- Was there a reduction? Of time or cost?
- Did you create savings? Of time or money?

Now, go back to the beginning of your journal and quantify. You can evaluate all of your accomplishments or just a few, I want you to practice thinking about what value you deliver and have added to your organization. Some quantification will only require numbers. Think about how many phone calls you took, how many members were on your team, how many dollars in your budget, or how many projects you led.

Others will require you to compare, such as delivering a 10% improvement or a 25% savings. Did you reduce talk time by 10 bps or 15 seconds? Did you exceed the goal by 20%? Perhaps you saved $550K by selecting a new vendor.

You can measure in time whether you saved 55 payroll hours, reduced average answer speed by 15 seconds, or submitted a project deliverable over a week early.

Wow - Look at all you have done! I encourage you to reflect on how you feel about your success. What comes up for you seeing these numbers? Which one of your contributions are you most proud of? What achievements will you build upon in the upcoming month and year?

Becoming good at recognizing your success and articulating the value delivered is a worthwhile skill. It may feel uncomfortable when you start, but once you find your stride, it will be something you do with ease. Practicing this now will also make updating or creating a résumé much more manageable when it is time. This process of quantifying success builds on itself, so getting good at this part will prepare you when we work on the next level.

BUILD + GROW HABITS
CIRCLE OF INFLUENCE
EXPAND YOUR CIRCLE

You have already been nurturing existing relationships daily. I hope you are finding satisfaction in reconnecting with people you enjoy. Let's build on that foundational habit.

When did you last hear someone say this job is an "individual contributor" role? It was probably not very long ago.

In my mind, nothing in work or life is truly something that can be done alone. Even individual contributors are part of a larger team. They may not have direct reports, but they work as part of a team on group projects or collaborate toward larger goals alongside their peers.

Now that we agree that we need others to perform at our collective best, let's discuss expanding our circle.

There are countless ways to meet new people, especially in a professional setting. Let's explore some effective, low-stress ways!

Attend Events:

Meeting people in a post-pandemic world is as easy as ever! There are many events available. Find what interests you either virtually or in person. Here are some of my favorite places to find new events:

- LinkedIn Events
- Facebook Events
- Social Media Groups
- Eventbrite
- Meetup
- Industry Events
- Fundraising Events

When you meet people virtually, make it super-easy for others to connect with you. Have a brief introduction with your name and social media links ready on a digital note so you can copy and paste it easily into the chat box. Below is a template you can use for this purpose:

Hello! I am [First Name + Last Name]. I am looking to expand my network. Let's connect on [social media platform name]. You can find me here [insert social media URL].

Connect with all the others that share their information, too. Be sure to save the chat from the meeting. This will allow you to contact those in attendance without missing out on what happens during the event.

For an in-person event, always take a friend or colleague with you. This way, you have someone familiar with you should you need their support. Meet new people by introducing yourself. Have a natural conversation with the person you are standing in line with or sitting next to. Make it easy to connect by having a business card handy or using a QR code to trade contact information. I love using my LinkedIn QR code. You can even save it as a photo on your phone so you can access it quickly when needed.

Ready to take action? Please find one in-person and one virtual event to attend this month. Do this every month to grow your circle. Record the events you plan to participate in right in your journal and then return to the journal and note who you met there and what you learned.

You have the tools to nurture and expand your circle of influence. Take a step further and learn my complete 5-5-5-5 Networking Method, where you will enhance the skills that will help you own your career and be a resource for others. Visit the *Own Your Career* resource portal by scanning the QR Code below to learn and implement the process.

The growth you experience in these Build + Grow Habits pages will prepare you to build self-confidence in your abilities and achievements, understand your worth, and grow your positive mindset and network. This is a pivotal next step in your career. Even if your career is not linear (mine wasn't either), you are making progress towards your goals and dreams. You are preparing yourself for unlocking the next level. You are doing amazing!

SECTION THREE

LEVELING UP HABITS

LEVELING UP HABITS

L eveling up can happen anywhere along your professional path. Maybe you're looking towards that promotion or a lateral move that will help you learn something new. You may receive a tap on your shoulder asking you to fill in for your manager when they are out of the office or taking a leave of absence. You could even be pursuing a certificate or furthering your education. Opportunities to level up come up when they are least expected, and I encourage you to welcome the chance with curiosity and decide whether it is for you. If you feel called, don't ignore it; explore it.

LEVELING UP HABITS
PERSONAL DEVELOPMENT
BUILD A PERSONAL USER MANUAL

I was introduced to the Personal User Manual concept in two LinkedIn articles by Aaron Hurst in 2013. Over the last 10+ years, I have used this concept in work settings with my direct teams and with leaders to whom I have reported. I use this framework with my clients when they are ready to transition into their new roles. It can also work for you in your current role or a brand-new one.

What is a Personal User Manual? This manual is a communication tool. Use it to document your preferences when working with others, set clear expectations, and learn how to meet the needs of those around you. The manual can contain any relevant data points that will help others work well with you.

To develop your Personal User Manual, make an initial pass at answering the questions below. Skip any that don't apply and add new questions specific to your circumstances.

Then, ask a trusted colleague or mentor to look at it for you. Do they feel you were being honest and that your Personal User Manual best reflects your work style? Listen openly to their feedback.

Refine your answers, then discuss them candidly with your direct reports, peers and leadership team. Make your answers accessible to coworkers as a reference document. Most importantly, invite those you work with to do the same. Knowing what makes people tick is the secret ingredient to productive collaborations and achieving common goals.

Values:

- List up to five top values. When considering your values, answer these questions.
- Do these values define me?
- Are these values a part of who I am?
- Do I use these values as a lens or a filter when making decisions?

Work Identity + Style:

- When I think about my role, do I see myself as an individual contributor or leader?
- If a leader, what is my leadership style?
- What is my work style?
- What activities bring me energy? What activities do I need more support around?

Communication:

- How do I prefer to be communicated with?
- When do I like people to approach me? How should others approach me?
- What is my preferred method of communicating with others?
- What is the worst way to communicate with me?
- These are some of my communication boundaries (Considerations may include the time of day, preferred method, or the flow, and frequency of communications).

Influence + Thought Leadership:

- How do I receive information?
- How do I make decisions?
- What do I stand for?
- What am I unwilling to tolerate?

What's Next:

- How do I envision team goals being achieved?
- What is my overall vision for the team I lead (or am part of) for the next year, three years, etc?
- What are my career goals for the next year, three years, etc?

Now that your Personal User Manual draft is ready to share, visit the *Own Your Career* resource portal and download a template to share a beautiful and thoughtful document with your team. Scan the QR code below to start.

LEVELING UP HABITS
KNOW YOUR WORTH
PREPARE FOR YOUR
PERFORMANCE REVIEW

W ould you rather hide under the desk than complete the self-evaluation part of a performance review? If you raised your hand, you are not alone. For most people, it is a dreaded work task.

Good news, it doesn't have to be! You made it this far in the book and invested in your career. You want to grow your skills and competencies. A performance review is one of the best times to demonstrate your professional evolution. I recommend you do that with achievements based on success metrics. Stories, data, and numbers are your best indicators.

Data and numbers are easy for you; you have been tracking your successes and quantifying them as part of the Know Your Worth sections of the foundational and build + grow habits. Now it's time to talk about those numbers in an engaging way, weave a story about how it all came together, and talk about the process and any lessons learned.

Select up to five examples of your professional growth from the past year. These examples should be tied to your performance metrics and match competency expectations for your level in the organization. To find the best examples, reference your work calendar, project updates, one-on-one meeting agendas, and the daily/weekly success files you've been creating.

Now that you have the metrics, competencies, and projects you are ready to discuss, grab your journal or blank document and brain dump. For everything that comes to mind, get it down. Do not edit yourself at this point. Don't judge what is coming from your heart to the page...let it flow.

I am sure you were able to capture more than you needed, so now it's time to edit. Stories are so much easier to share when you use an engaging framework. I recommend an interview storytelling style that will condense your experiences into a concise and impactful narrative.

Think of these stories like Instagram Reels or YouTube Shorts. They are catchy, grab interest, and deliver the "Wow!" factor.

Use the **STAR** method.

- S - Situation
- T - Task
- A - Action
- R - Result and Reflection

I used to train hiring managers on the STAR technique when I was a Training Manager early in my career. Bringing this information to you now feels like a full circle moment. Storytelling is a skill that will serve you well in all areas and at all levels in your professional life. Master this competency now and others will lean when you speak.

Visit the *Own Your Career* resource portal to access the STAR method framework and architect impactful stories for your performance review. To learn more *about the* STAR method, scan the QR code below.

LEVELING UP HABITS
MINDSET
VISIONING

"Visualization is the practice of repeatedly imagining what you want to achieve in order to create it and attract it."
-Inc Magazine[vi]

Perhaps you already subscribe to ideas like the law of attraction, manifestation, putting things out into the universe, or a higher power or purpose.

Olympic athletes use the practice of visualization to help them achieve their goals, including swimmers Katie Ledecky and Michael Phelps and ski powerhouse Lindsey Vonn. Spanx founder Sarah Blakely is also known to use visualization to reach her aspirations.

To visualize success, let's discuss creating a vision board, which can be a tool for helping you build and attract what you want for yourself and your career.

To inspire you to come up with your powerful vision, answer these questions:

Vision:

- What does your best self look like?
- Think vividly here: how does your ideal self dress? Walk? Talk?
- What does she do with her free time? Go deep here; your future self will thank you.

Goals:

- What goals, once achieved, will help you become that version of yourself?
- In addition to your career and work goals, consider goals focused on health, wealth, relationships, spirituality, knowledge building, travel, experiences, family, and fun.

Actions:

- What behaviors and habits will help you achieve these goals?
- How does your best self spend her time? What does she do every day?
- How does she move in this world?

Create

Based on the vision, goals, and actions you clarified above, select physical and visual representations of them for your board. Consider using:

- Words (quotes, headline clippings from magazines and whole passages from books)
- Images (stock photos, search images, and printed pics from your camera roll)
- Colors (bright and bold, soft and subtle, or using colors to convey feelings and emotions)

Now that you have a direction for your vision bring it to life. Will you make a tangible vision board on paper? Use some of your craft supply stash? Or will you opt for a digital board you can look at in your camera roll whenever the feeling strikes you? There's no correct answer; choose what feels authentic for you right now. Happy creating!

Access a digital vision board template by scanning the QR code below and visiting the *Own Your Career* resource portal.

LEVELING UP HABITS
CIRCLE OF INFLUENCE
REVIEW PROFESSIONAL
RELATIONSHIPS

Work relationships are valuable. Gallup results show that highly engaged individuals have better outcomes when they have a best friend at work.[vii]

I have made deep and lifelong friendships with people I met at work. You know who you are.

Make a list of the people you spend the most time with. For this exercise, focus on your professional relationships.

Have your list?

Now consider the impact these individuals have on you. Ask yourself the following questions.

- Do they contribute to your positive mindset?
- Do they cheer you on in achieving your stretch goals?
- Do they contribute to your personal and professional development?
- Do they support you in finding solutions for workplace problems?

If anyone on your list caused you to answer "no" to any of the above questions, or your work bestie is jealous of your accomplishments, sabotages your success, and has nothing nice to say about anyone...ever, I encourage you to reconsider the relationship. Lay a healthy boundary on how you prefer to interact with this person at work and outside the office.

You've undoubtedly seen the quote on social media with the phrasing, "Sit with winners. The conversation is different." If you find yourself having the same conversation every day, you may need a different set of people at your table.

LEVELING UP HABITS
ACCOMPLISHMENT
SHOW UP AS HER

A few pages back, I walked you through an exercise on how to envision the best version of you. Showing up as her, the future you, is taking your vision to the next level. You get to be her. Embody her.

This is not faking it 'til you make it. This is you acknowledging that you are already the person you wish to become. This version of you already exists, and you decide to be her in various ways.

More than anything, this is a way of being. This is your presence in the world. Maybe you have heard of it as the "it factor." Some may refer to it as executive presence. It is a part of your emotional intelligence.

How do you focus on building your presence to show up as the best version of you? In recent months, I have learned that it is about pause. Before you speak, react, or respond, take a deep breath, pause, and give yourself time to formulate what is next. You could even whisper to yourself, "How would the best version of myself respond?" "What would my future self do in this situation?"

To show up as my best self, on weekdays, I wake up and prepare for my day by getting ready. That means getting dressed in my version of business casual, usually a dress and super fun necklace, and doing my hair and applying my makeup. I don't do these things for external validation. I do them to feel ready to meet with clients, collaborators, and partners. It puts my brain in "professional" mode, and I can be the best coach, mentor, and value-added partner possible. And I continue to practice how I show up every day. It is an ever-evolving skill.

A quick note about the imposter phenomenon here: just because you are trying something new doesn't mean you won't figure it out. It doesn't mean you are making a big mistake. No one is going to walk up to you and say, "You don't belong here." "Who do you think you are?" "You are a fraud!"

If you hear those phrases in your mind, recognize that voice for what it is: your inner critic. That voice is the opposite of your best self. This is the voice that wants to keep you small. Just like you will pause when you want to get in touch with the best version of you, pause and notice that inner critical voice. And then dismiss it. If you haven't already watched Reshma Saujani's Smith College Commencement Address, *Imposter Syndrome Is A Scheme*, you should.[viii] It transformed my view on imposter syndrome, and I think you will also appreciate her unique perspective.

Showing up as her is an advanced habit to develop. I invite you to explore methods that could work for you and have fun trying different things.

Track in your journal what methods work well for you. Record the technique you used, the circumstances, and what felt right about the approach. Build on your successes and then refine your approach.

Guess what?

You did it – you leveled up! You should be proud of yourself for trying new things and expanding how you think about yourself and your mindset. Your circle of influence is growing and getting stronger with continued connection.

By investing in your development, you are gaining a more profound knowledge of things that interest you, building skills, and increasing your value. You now know your worth at work and in the overall market and have the research and data to back it up.

Most importantly, you have learned how to track your accomplishments, quantify those achievements, and tell impactful stories about your successes. You no longer downplay your contributions. I see you, and you are just getting started!

NEXT STEPS

Managing your career is not something that was taught in school. Although it should be! Your employer doesn't require you to take an eLearning module during an annual compliance training. At the bare minimum, your leader may be invested in their team members, and they may have a conversation with you during performance review time.

You have taken the initial steps forward by securing and following the roadmap I used to build and level up my own corporate career.

You now have the tools to develop a positive mindset, which include practicing daily gratitude, speaking to yourself gently using affirmations, and envisioning and embodying your vision.

You're investing in your personal and professional development by reading to expand your mind, leveraging your company's educational offerings, and sharing a personal user manual to build a stronger interpersonal communication style.

You have learned how to track and quantify your successes and show up as her, the absolute best version of you.

Certainly, no easy task, you understand and know your worth through careful calculations and research within your company and the broader market. You are ready to articulate this value during your performance review! Look at you!

Lastly, you are staying in contact with your most valuable asset, your network, building new connections, and evaluating who surrounds you, ensuring they are supportive and interested in your continued growth.

You have come so far already. Do any of these statements sound like you?

I am ready for more.

I know my worth and I am ready to add the tax.

I deserve the support to go after my dreams.

I am ready to start now.

I own my career!

If you are ready to take your career beyond what you imagined before picking up this book...then you are in the right place. You are right on time. You don't have to go after your professional dreams alone.

I invite you to join me in a community of women just like you as we build a safe place to be you. Talk about your career, share success, and work through challenges. I welcome you because what you have to offer is what is needed. Expand your network with others who are walking the same path as you. Let's discover our possibilities together. I look forward to seeing you there!

To accept your invitation to join the **Own Your Career Community**, scan the QR code below.

Annette Garsteck

ACKNOWLEDGEMENTS

A heartfelt thank you to all the women who have invested in me, my career, and my future. I appreciate all the sacrifices made that allowed me to step forward. I am grateful you reached out and extended your hand to pull me up to stand with you.

To my mom, Rosemary; my godmother, Annette; and my sister, Lisa, you are there for me every day, and I couldn't be more grateful for you. To my brother, Tom, you have always been a strong support, and I thank you. Thank you to my mother-in-law, Dorothy, who always tells everyone I am *her* daughter.

To all of my dear friends (listed alphabetically, to be fair): Amy, Andrea, Ann, Carolyn, Gayle, Jasmin, Jessica, Katie, Kori, Larissa, Lindsay, Lisa, Portia, Sandra, and Valerie, thank you for listening to me when I am trying to work out an idea or a problem. Know that I am so happy to be in your circle.

To the women who inspire me as entrepreneurs, I am grateful for the time and knowledge you share with me, including those in Next Level CLE, Working Women Connection, Parisi Pack, Moxie Mastermind, WINCleveland, and the International Association of Career Coaches.

To all those who reported to me during my career in corporate America and those who have allowed me to guide them as their career coach, your career trajectories always amaze me. I am grateful to you for allowing me to walk alongside you and guide you on your professional path.

For my coaches, Cara, Sherri, Steph, Sara, Jen, Jennah, Shannon, and Val, sharing your zone of genius has helped me find mine. Thank you for pouring into me.

Lastly, a very special thank you to my loving husband, Ray, who has always seen my potential and encouraged me to follow my dreams, desires, and passions, even when the ideas seemed like a big stretch. It is comforting to have you alongside me every step of life's journey. 🤍

ABOUT THE AUTHOR

When Annette Garsteck gave her two weeks' notice and left corporate America in 2015, she knew she was ready to do her own thing but wasn't quite sure yet what that might look like. Her husband, Ray, had a brilliant idea: "Why don't you write résumés?"

Nearly a decade later, the seed Ray planted has blossomed into Annette Garsteck Career Consulting—a thriving small business that has helped hundreds of happy clients reinvent their careers and fall in love with their work lives.

As an International Association of Career Coaches-credentialed Senior Professional Career Coach and Senior Professional Résumé Writer, Annette has become a trusted and visible resource in the career development space. She is the cohost of "Exposing the Hidden Reality" weekly live conversation and has been featured in SUCCESS Magazine, Fast Company, BBC, and more.

Having spent nearly two decades in corporate America, Annette often calls on her background as a hiring manager and leader in Fortune 50 and world-class healthcare firms in her work with clients. Her unique vantage point from her past work life provides an insider's playbook for jobseekers and career professionals looking to be noticed, advocate for themselves—and get hired.

Annette resides in Northeast Ohio with Ray and their perky Pomeranian, Claire. She's rarely without a book in hand, and she is excited to add her own book to the ever-growing collection.

SUPPORTING RESOURCES

T hank you to the many sources of inspiration and information I have quoted and referenced in this book. I have cited them below, feel free to explore them to learn more.

[i] Wikimedia Foundation. (2024, January 28). *Personal development*. Wikipedia. https://en.wikipedia.org/wiki/Personal_develo pment#cite_note-1

[ii] Sussex Publishers. (2024, December 28). *Self-talk*. Psychology Today. https://www.psychologytoday.com/us/basics/ self-talk

[iii] Kaado, B. (2024, February 28). *Why reading is good for your career and business*. Business News Daily. https://www.businessnewsdaily.com/9998- reading-helps-career.html

[iv] CBS Evening News. (2025, January 15.). *Sheryl Sandberg pushes women to "lean in."* YouTube. https://www.youtube.com/watch?v=st5j- 84MGG0

[v] Moore, C. (2024, December 24.). *Positive daily affirmations: Is there science behind it?.* PositivePsychology.com. https://positivepsychology.com/daily-affirmations/#science

[vi] Rovello, J. (2024, February 28). *5 ways Katie Ledecky, Michael Phelps, and other Olympians visualize success.* Inc.com. https://www.inc.com/jessica-rovello/five-steps-to-visualize-success-like-an-olympian.html

[vii] Patel, A., & Plowman, S. (2024, January 22). *The increasing importance of a best friend at work.* Gallup.com. https://www.gallup.com/workplace/397058/increasing-importance-best-friend-work.aspx

[viii] Saujani, R. (2024, October 10). *Imposter Syndrome Is A Scheme.* YouTube. https://www.youtube.com/watch?v=BoHDDgeQtlc&t=2s

Photo of Annette Garsteck by Katie Garlock

Made in United States
Cleveland, OH
02 February 2025

13989493R10044